W9-BBW-191

# Ask And It Shall Be Given

BY Donald T. Kauffman

THE C. R. GIBSON COMPANY

Norwalk, Connecticut 06856

ACKNOWLEDGMENTS

All Scripture quotations in this publication, unless otherwise indicated, are from the Holy Bible, New International Version. Copyright © 1973, 1978, 1984, International Bible Society.

The quotation from Frank C. Laubach is used by permission of Robert S. Laubach, son of the author Frank C. Laubach (1884-1970).

The quotation condensed from *The Fourth Dimension* (Bridge Publishing, Inc.) is used by permission of the author, Paul Yonggi Cho.

The quotation by S. E. McMillen from *None Of These Diseases* is used by permission of Fleming H. Revell, publisher.

*To my wife, Jeanne*

❀

*"Ask and it will be given to you; seek and you will find; knock and the door will be opened to you. For everyone who asks receives; he who seeks finds; and to him who knocks, the door will be opened. Which of you, if his son asks for bread, will give him a stone? Or if he asks for a fish will give him a snake? If you, then, though you are evil, know how to give good gifts to your children, how much more will your Father in heaven give good gifts to those who ask him!"*

Matthew 7:7-11

❀

# THE POWER OF PRAYER

❀

THE mysterious but mighty power of prayer is being re-discovered by our generation. Ruth and Susan were deeply concerned about their church. Attendance and interest had sunk to such a low ebb that when Ruth was told no one wanted to serve on most of the committees, her first thought was: *Why should they?*

But even though both women felt their church situation was almost hopeless, they agreed to pray about it. Then, as they continued to pray and talk, ideas began to flow. They planned a special meeting, open by invitation only. Rumors (which Ruth and Susan helped plant) spread about the importance of the meeting, and eventually every last member of the church they had hoped would come, was there.

Everyone was given a copy of the Prayer of St. Francis and asked to underline the three lines that spoke most directly to her or him. Finally they were asked to name their interests and goals for their church, and what they would like to contribute.

Before the meeting was over, every opening on every

committee was filled, and there were beginnings of fascinating new projects which no one had thought of before! Best of all, the pastor, who had been written off by some of the members as cold and uncaring, was invited to join a small prayer group Ruth and Susan started. They learned that their minister was just as concerned about the church as they were—perhaps even more concerned—but he had been unable to break through the church's weight of tradition and reserve.

Prayer melted the reserve; prayer paved the way for new ideas; prayer proved once again to have a unique power to release the creative Presence of the One who is "able to do immeasurably more than all we ask or imagine." (Ephesians 3:20)

Prayer has many forms. It may be purely praise and thanksgiving. Sometimes it is simply fellowship with our Lord, neither asking nor expecting anything but a sense of His caring love. It may take the shape of affirmation or meditation. Prayer does not need to "get results."

Nevertheless, there is such a thing as praying with power. St. James wrote, "The prayer of a righteous man is powerful and effective." (James 5:16) And when Jesus had performed a spectacular healing and the disciples asked why they had not been able to do anything, He answered "This kind can come out only by prayer." (Mark 9:29)

The seven steps that follow are designed to help you develop power in prayer. As you take these steps one after another, you will find yourself walking in a sometimes strange, but always marvelously exciting, world. You will know, in your own experience, the certainty of this promise: "Ask and it will be given to you; seek and you will find; knock and the door will be opened to you." (Matthew 7:7)

# FIND YOUR SECRET PLACE

*In the castle of my soul
Is a little postern gate,
Whereat, when I enter,
I am in the presence of God.*
Walter Rauschenbusch

❊

THERE are no precise rules for prayer. We can pray anywhere, at any time, in practically every conceivable situation. But it is helpful for most of us who long for the presence and power of God to prepare our thoughts and hearts for Him. Those of us who try to exercise regularly know how important it is to warm up before we begin. Much more importantly, we can prepare ourselves for prayer by taking the steps to warm our cold hearts and flex our spiritual capacities.

Most Christians can recite the Lord's Prayer. What we sometimes forget is that before Jesus gave those match-less words, He said, "When you pray, go into your room, close the door and pray to your Father, who is unseen." (Matthew 6:6) In other words, before you pray, find a time and a place to turn aside from the worries and concerns of everyday life and concentrate on God alone and His love and power.

Jesus set the example. Often His disciples learned that He had slipped away early in the morning to go out into the hills where He could be alone with His heavenly Father.

Where is your secret place? You may want to set apart a special chair or area for this purpose. For some a framed verse of Scripture, a picture or a cross is helpful for drawing our thoughts toward God. A chapel I like has a stained-glass window of the Good Shepherd tending his flock. It reminds me of our Lord's incredible loving care for each one of His sometimes silly, often straying, always needy sheep.

When the members of one small group were asked when and where they prayed, the women gave various answers. Nearly all the men said they prayed most often in their cars on the way to or from work. Centuries ago Brother Lawrence testified that he prayed as easily at his duties in the kitchen of his monastery as anywhere else. He had found the gate "in the castle of his soul" that opens into the Kingdom. Our secret place can be anywhere, but for many it is helpful to find a special place to be alone.

Your may want to dedicate a special time to pray. For many, an ideal time is the first half hour or so in the morning or the last minutes before bedtime. Choose your own time, but set it apart regularly until your moments with God become a vital part of your life.

*Every morning lean thine arms awhile*
*Upon the window sill of heaven*
*And gaze upon thy Lord.*
*Then, with the vision in thy heart,*
*Turn strong to meet thy day.*
                                        Author Unknown

"Close the door...." Deliberately clear your mind of all the things that usually demand your attention. Shut your eyes if this helps shut out the clamor of the world. Try sitting in a comfortable chair in as relaxed a manner as possible. You may find soft music useful to create a sound screen behind which you can draw more fully into the secret place.

Then try one or two of these ideas:

Read Psalm 91. Think about the promise in verse 1 for the person who dwells "in the secret place." What other promises in this psalm can you claim as your own?

Read Psalm 23 and mentally picture yourself as a lamb nestled in the loving arms of the Good Shepherd. Feel His love surrounding you, holding you tight.

Now you are ready to bring your needs to Him.

John Greenleaf Whittier had this to say about his secret place:

> And so I find it well to come
> For deeper rest to this small room
> For here the habit of the soul
> Feels less the outer world's control;
> The world that time and sense have known
> Falls off and leaves us God alone.

THANK YOU, LORD, for all the good gifts and all the time You give me. Accept this time I set apart for You as my special gift to You. Help me to draw near to You. For I know that You have already drawn close to me. You are waiting for me to enter into the wonderful fellowship we can have together through Jesus Christ.                          AMEN

# TALK WITH GOD

*Thou art coming to a King,*
*Large petitions with thee bring*
*For His grace and power are such*
*None can ever ask too much.*

John Newton

A MARRIAGE counselor who was being interviewed on a television program said that four elements are necessary for a good relationship: time, talk, truth and trust. If talk is important in a friendship or a marriage, how much more important it is in developing a relationship with the One who invites: "If you...know how to give good gifts to your children, how much more will your Father in heaven give good gifts to those who ask him!" (Matthew 7:11)

It may seem too, too simple to say that in praying we should talk with God. But how often do we forget to do exactly that?

I do. Late one afternoon my family and I were returning to our New Jersey home from a visit to my brother in up-state New York. There was not even a barn in sight when the steering wheel told me something was wrong, and we soon discovered we had a flat tire.

With the old wrench, I could not budge a single nut on the wheel with the flat. After the wrench had slipped off the rusty nut for what seemed like the zillionth time, I prayed. My prayer was not theological but it was very short and very fervent: "Lord, please help us!" Then one of the nuts moved slightly. Then another. And the tire was changed and we were safely on our way home.

I often wonder why I wait until things are desperate before asking God for help. I am trying to learn to talk to God more consistently. But I can testify that time after time, in spite of my bad manners toward God, He has answered.

You may feel it is rather presumptious to ask the Creator of the universe, whose suns and galaxies no human has yet been able to count, to concern Himself with our small affairs. But if He is our father, He has to care about everything in our lives. And He is big enough to handle the universe and our problems, too!

If we human parents, whose love for our children is often so misguided and imperfect, care as we do about each one of our children and grandchildren, how much more, Jesus assures us, will our heavenly Father give us the good things we ask for.

But we may wonder if it isn't selfish to ask God for things for ourselves. Shouldn't we be praying for other people instead? Maybe it's not a question of either/or. Let's take a look at the Lord's Prayer. Remember, this is the prayer Jesus gave His disciples when they asked Him to teach them to pray. In it we ask for all the basic things we need.

Give us this day our daily bread...We are invited to ask for the food we need, for anything essential. And forgive... God is waiting for us to ask for the healing of our mistakes, our old sins and guilt and troubling memories—one of our deepest needs. Here we learn that such healing and forgiveness depend on whether we truly forgive others. And lead...God knows we need His guidance. He waits patiently for us to ask Him to lead us through the dangerous trials and pitfalls of life, finally to deliver us from evil.

Praying for what we need helps us learn to pray effectively for others. As we ask our Father to fill our own needs of maintenance, peace and guidance, we are encouraged to pray for others' needs, too. God leads us to love our brothers and sisters in the same manner that we love and take care of ourselves.

*"Speak to Him, thou, for He hears,*
*and spirit with Spirit can meet—*
*Closer is He than breathing,*
*and nearer than hands and feet."*
Alfred Tennyson

Here are some things to do:

Try *writing* some of your prayers. One man has been doing this for many years. Each day he writes a letter to his Lord, and his serene faith is testimony that he has benefited from putting his prayers on paper.

*Read* some prayers. You will find some heart—tugging ones in the Bible, especially in the Psalms. There is marvelous food for thought and meditation in some of the great prayers of the church and of saintly men and women through the centuries.

Use *music*. My daughter Nancy tells me she often finds fresh inspiration for prayer from reading a good hymn or listening to a recording of songs of praise. In all our praying, let us not forget to praise and thank the One who has done so much for us.

But whatever you do, let nothing keep you from *speaking*—either aloud or silently—to your Father and Friend in your own words. Speak simply; you do not need to impress God with big words or eloquent diction. Speak confidently, trustingly, expectantly. Lay bare your heart to the One who loves you most.

> *Lord, teach me to silence my own heart that I may listen to the gentle movement of the Holy Spirit within me and sense the depths which are of God.* Sixteenth Century German Prayer

FATHER, teach me to pray. Help me to learn to trust You for all my needs, large or small. I cast all my care on You, for I know that You care deeply for me. Thank you for Your immeasurable love. AMEN

# EXPECT GREAT THINGS FROM GOD

> *Expect great things from God;*
> *attempt great things for God.*
> William Carey

❀

I her fine book *A Wide Place for My Steps* Elizabeth Rockwood asks, "Does anything happen when you pray?" Things are not likely to happen unless we have great expectations.

There are some remarkable passages in the Gospels about the importance of believing, hoping, expecting God to respond in some definite way to our prayers. Once when Jesus returned to the area where He had spent His early life, some of the neighbors said in effect, "We know him—he's just a carpenter's son!" As a result He "did not do many miracles there, because of their lack of faith." (Matthew 13:58) It appears that Jesus' countrymen's lack of faith virtually tied His hands. Later, when our Lord found a fig tree without fruit, He commanded that no one ever eat fruit from it again. The next day the disciples noticed that the tree had withered. When they asked Him about this, Jesus replied:

"Have faith in God....I tell you the truth, if anyone says to this mountain, 'Go throw yourself into the sea,' and does not doubt in his heart but believes that what he says will happen, it will be done for him. Therefore I tell you, whatever you ask for in prayer, believe that you have received it, and it will be yours." (Mark 11:22–24)

There are two important conditions here. First, Jesus emphasized the importance of not doubting in the heart —of believing without reservation, refusing to doubt right down in the center of our being. Second, He tells us to believe that we have already received what we ask for, and He promises that then it will be ours.

How do you exercise faith like that? One way is to picture to yourself what you are asking for, just as vividly and concretely as possible, even to the extent of believing that the result we desire is already ours!

The power of such "imaging" is being demonstrated today in scientific circles. A British doctor recommends this procedure for setting the healing process in one's body in motion:

Relax in an easy chair until every part of the body has lost its tension and you can begin to hear your own heartbeat. Picture yourself in some pleasant, secure situation— for example, bask mentally in the sun on an uncrowded seashore.

Then visualize whatever part of your body needs attention, returning to full health. Let's say your toe is broken. Picture the blood carrying calcium to the broken bone, the break mending, the toe returning to full normal vigor. Continue imaging this for perhaps twenty minutes, twice a day.

There is increasing evidence that such a procedure will immeasurably augment the healing forces which God has put within our bodies. And there are more and more amazing examples of the beneficial physical benefits of positive imagination accompanied by Christian faith and prayer.

One notable example is Harry DeCamp, a New Jersey sales executive who learned that he was the victim of inoperable cancer. He went home from the hospital to die; he remembers that when he asked the physician in charge how much time he had left, the doctor answered, "No time."

But someone sent Harry a card containing the words, "With God all things are possible," and Harry wondered if it was possible for his cancer to be healed. He had no idea how to pray, but he pictured God sitting beside him, and he asked Him to heal him.

And Harry began picturing to himself the white blood cells in his blood coursing through his system and destroying the cancer cells. Somehow, as he played this scene over and over on the screen of his imagination, he saw Jesus Christ leading the attack on the cancer cells. "Where did He come from?" Harry wondered. But after that He was there each time he pictured that scene.

A day came when Harry knew in his heart that he had been healed. During his illness he had vowed that if he recovered he would "shout the story from the housetops," and he has never refused an invitation to tell his amazing story. I have heard him tell it a number of times, and it is a heart-wrenching experience to see this big specimen of perfect health struggle to get out the words to tell what

God has done. Medical tests have repeatedly confirmed Harry's healing. In the eight years since his remarkable experience, no trace of cancer has been found.

When you pray, believe as deeply and sincerely as you can that God will answer. Try this:

Picture to yourself as clearly as possible exactly what you would like God to do for you. Make the picture specific and concrete. Fill in all the details.

Write down exactly what you want. Write out each detail. Write down a time when you expect the answer to come.

At least once each day sit down, relax, shut your eyes and picture the answer to your prayer. Hold the image in your mind and heart, imagining what you desire coming to pass.

One young woman had a number of desires. She wanted a good relationship with another person. She wanted a good home with a fireplace. She wanted to become less of an introvert and to have some good friends. She wrote all this down and gave it to a friend.

Six months later her friend mailed her letter back. She was rather amazed to review all that had happened. She now had a number of friends, one a specially good one, and she was living in a beautiful home with not one but two fireplaces!

"If any of you lacks wisdom," wrote St. James, "he should ask God who gives generously to all without finding fault, and it will be given to him. But when he asks, he must believe and not doubt, because he who doubts is like a wave of the sea, blown and tossed by the wind. That man should not think he will receive anything from the

Lord; he is a double-minded man, unstable in all he does."
(James 1:5–8)

We do not need to understand every word of this passage perfectly to realize that God is a generous Giver and that His gifts come to us through the channel of believing prayer. The more strongly and clearly we believe, the more surely we can expect answers to our prayers.

> *There is an "Archimedian" point outside the world which is the little chamber where a true suppliant prays in all sincerity, where he lifts the world off its hinges.* Sören Kierkegaard

FATHER, every good and perfect gift is in Your hand, waiting for me to claim. Help me to be bold and strong in faith until Your answer comes. AMEN

# LET GO AND LET GOD

> *Drop thy still dews of quietness,*
> *Till all our strivings cease;*
> *Take from our souls the strain and stress,*
> *And let our ordered lives confess*
> *The beauty of thy peace.*
> John Greenleaf Whittier

❧

A CANADIAN chemist named Albert Cliffe, who made some exciting spiritual discoveries, titled one of his books *Let Go and Let God*. This aptly expresses the fact that we need to get out of the way so that we do not hinder God from answering our prayers. When we learn to let go of our problems and turn them over to God, we have taken an important step toward spiritual power.

A mother learned this when she met with a prayer partner to pray about her grown son. She had worried for years about his personal habits, his seeming immaturity, his dropping out of school and failure to hold a job.

When she told the partner her prayer concerns, he suggested a period of silence before the Lord. Then he said: "I am getting the picture that for years you have been like someone hanging by the fingertips from a cliff. You can't hang on much longer. You're about to drop. The message I have for you is: Drop!"

The mother went home realizing that she had been too possessive. She tried to stop worrying about her son and to turn him over to God. She stopped criticizing. And she was pleasantly surprised when her son of his own accord dropped most of the habits that had concerned her, applied for a student loan, went back to school, and demonstrated the fact that he was well on the way to successful maturity.

Let go and let God. When you pray you may become aware of some obstruction in your life to the flow of God's love and power. The Psalmist wrote long ago: "If I had cherished sin in my heart, the Lord would not have listened." (Psalm 66:18) Hugging anything wrong can prevent God's answers from reaching us.

Why is this? Someone has compared the presence of wrong desires or attitudes in our lives to hanging clothes on a television antenna. Sin is often no more than something good in the wrong place. There is nothing wrong with hanging out laundry to dry in the sun, but we cannot hang it on the TV antenna and expect good reception!

If you become aware of something wrong in your life, bring it to the gracious God of all mercy. Ask Him to help you put it behind you.

Try this:

As you pray, drop your hands to your sides, fingers open, to symbolize the fact that you are letting go and casting all your anxiety on Him. Let God have the problem you have brought to Him. Say to yourself, "I have committed this to God. I will not worry about it again. Instead I will trust Him to solve it, or else to show me how to begin to help answer my own prayer."

Now open your hands and hold them cupped in your lap. Ask God to fill your life with His goodness and peace. Try to feel His good gifts filling your hands to overflowing.

Ask yourself whether you are doing anything to hinder God from giving you His best.

CREATE in me a clean heart, O God, and renew a right spirit within me. Help me to see if I am somehow hindering Your work. Let me move forward spiritually. Help me let go and let God. AMEN

# OPEN THE CHANNEL

*And when you stand praying, if you hold anything against anyone, forgive him, so that your Father in heaven may forgive you your sins.*

*Mark 11:25*

❀

SOMEONE has observed that our Lord talked about one thing more than any other in connection with prayer. We might expect this to be faith, but it is not. The one thing Jesus emphasized more than anything else when He talked about praying was the importance of having a forgiving spirit. After He had given His followers the Lord's Prayer, Jesus reemphasized this one so important part of it:

"For if you forgive men when they sin against you, your heavenly Father will also forgive you. But if you do not forgive men their sins, your Father will not forgive your sins." (Matthew 6:14–15)

Evidently forgiveness is very important in effective prayer. Why? God is Love. Does resentment or ill will clog the channels of spiritual power that only total Love can open?

I learned an important lesson about this at a retreat in Massachusetts. During the retreat I had chest pains severe enough that when two sisters mentioned they had a healing ministry, I accepted their invitation to meet with them for prayer.

Margaret and Clara laid their hands on my head and asked when I had first noticed the chest pains. Their questions reminded me that it had been during a period of mental and spiritual anguish. I had been working at two jobs and was often away from my wife and family.

Margaret said, "Go back in your memory and say to your wife, 'Forgive me, Jeanne.' You hurt her, and you need to have the wound healed."

Sitting in a straight-backed chair with the two sisters' hands firmly on my head, I said, "Forgive me, Jeanne." Then I prayed and Margaret prayed for my forgiveness and healing, and I knew that Clara was praying silently.

I cannot explain what happened. I did not feel particularly different when the prayer with the sisters was over. But for the next three days I had the sensation that the hands of Jesus Christ were resting on my head. And the chest pains went away. And when I had my annual physical five months later, the cardiac irregularity that had been detected the year before was gone.

The medical world today is learning that there is a closer relationship than used to be realized between emotional and spiritual well being and physical health. We need not understand the laws of God to put them into practice. I have learned from my own experience that forgiveness is a vital part of health of body, mind and spirit.

Physician S. I. McMillen writes in his book *None of These Diseases*: "When Jesus said, 'Forgive...' He was thinking not only of our souls, but of saving our bodies from irritable bowel syndrome, coronary artery disease, high blood pressure, and many other diseases."

Science can detect the beneficial physical effects of forgiving. Acquiring power in prayer is one of its effects on the soul and spirit.

Exactly what is forgiveness? My dictionary tells me it means to cancel a debt or to cease to feel resentful. When I forgive someone, I mentally cross that person's debt off the ledgers of my memory and try to drop any resentment I may feel.

But I understood forgiveness better when I looked up the Greek word for it. Greek, of course, was the original language of the New Testament. In classical Greek *forgive* meant let go, give up, permit, tolerate or set free. It was used for letting a ship sail away, setting a horse loose, freeing a slave, discharging missiles or even for excusing someone from a flogging.

Basically, to forgive means to let go any ill will or bad feeling against another person—to drop that feeling, forget that bad memory, give it up and remember it no more!

I admit this is not at all easy to do, particularly if you feel the other person did something horribly wrong. But our Lord doesn't tell us to forgive nice actions. It's the worst ones that need the most forgiveness. We need to remember that our own record isn't perfect and that if we expect forgiveness for ourselves, we've got to extend it to others.

Of course, forgiving is a lot easier said than done. Corrie ten Boom, that remarkable Dutchwoman who was sent to a Nazi concentration camp for helping Jews in wartime Holland, found that out after she miraculously survived. Her father and sister died in the Nazi camps, but after the war Corrie felt a call to tell the Germans of the love and forgiveness of God.

One evening as she spoke, Corrie noticed in her audience one of the cruelest guards from Ravensbruck, where her sister Betsie had died. After the message, the guard came to her with a smile, talking glibly of God's love, and asked her to forgive him. When Corrie looked at this man, all she could see was the Nazi uniform he used to wear and her sister Betsie's slowly starving form.

Corrie ten Boom knew she ought to hold out her hand to take the guard's, but her hand would not move. Her whole body was frozen as she remembered the awful inhumanity of Ravensbruck. She felt she could never smile at this man who was smiling his "God forgives me and you should, too" smile at her.

She prayed: "Help me, Lord! I cannot love this man. I cannot even shake his hand. You love him through me."

And the miracle happened. Something more powerful than electricity surged through Corrie's hand as she felt it grasping his. She heard herself saying she loved him and forgave him. And she was freed for a marvelous, worldwide ministry of speaking and writing.

Try these things:

Whenever you become aware of ill will or resentment against anyone, consciously forgive and ask God to bless that person. Jesus was very clear on this: "Love your enemies, do good to those who hate you, bless those who curse you, pray for those who mistreat you." (Luke 6:27–28)

If the person you hold something against is within

reach, take him or her a present. It needn't be expensive. A home-baked pie can convey lots of love!

If the person is far away, write a letter. You may or may not want to formally write about forgiveness. Warm words of love and friendliness can break down barriers and heal your own spirit even if they don't change the other person.

What if the person you need to forgive is dead? Then sit down quietly, relax, and go back in your memory and forgive. Bitter memories can ruin your happiness. Healed ones—restored through active love and forgiveness—can bring you the peace and joy that this world can never take away.

LORD, make me an instrument of Your peace and love. Forbid that any other person should sour my spirit. Help me to forgive everyone in my circle of contacts so freely that Your love and joy overflow in everything I do.   AMEN

# STOP, LOOK AND LISTEN

*Lord, teach me to silence my
own heart that I may listen to
the gentle movement of the Holy
Spirit within me and sense the
depths which are of God.*

Sixteenth Century Prayer

WHEN we pray, one thing we need to do is simply to *stop*. Stop worrying. Stop letting our minds run in useless circles. Stop fruitless striving. Stop thinking we are all-sufficient. Stop talking.

And *look*. When the prophet Elisha was surrounded by a hostile army, he was unafraid, for he could see a far stronger army of "horses and chariots" which filled the mountains. And when he prayed for his servant, "Open his eyes so he may see," the servant also saw the army of the Lord. (II Kings 6:15, 17)

And we need to *listen*. When we learn to become quiet and to become aware of the dimensions beyond our own, we begin to "sense the depths which are of God."

Prayer brings vision and wisdom. Soon after my wife

and I moved to our present hometown in Connecticut, the water in our house stopped flowing. No one could figure out why. The man who had recently dug our well pulled up the pump, found everything in apparent order, and was baffled.

My wife, Jeanne, has the custom of beginning each day with a quiet time of prayer, Scripture reading and meditation. That morning she had not yet begun her quiet time when the well-digger arrived. After she greeted him and he began his examination of the water supply, she sat down to pray. Immediately an idea came to her. She asked the well-digger if there might be any connection between our water loss and the installation of our new telephone line the day before. That was it! A search revealed that the stake which had been driven in the earth to ground the telephone had split the power line for the well. A simple repair brought back our water.

Closing out the physical world for a time in prayer and opening our eyes to spiritual realities clears our vision and helps us listen. "Be silent," said Francois Fenelon, "and God will speak."

And Frank Laubach, who helped millions of people in various countries learn to read and to write, once said: "Prayer at its highest is a two-way conversation—and for me the most important part is listening to God's replies." Sometimes Laubach opened his mouth when he was praying and let God speak to him through his own tongue.

Here are some exercises:

Try it. Be quiet right now and say: "Father, what do you want me to do today? What is the next step I should take toward the solution of the problem I have laid before you?" Now let the answer come out of your own mouth.

And try this. In a notebook or on a piece of paper make three columns. Write your prayer requests in the first column, the things God seems to be saying to you in the second, and the final answer to each prayer in the third. After you have prayed, be sure to write in the second column what you believe God is telling you, or wants you to do, in response to your prayer.

Now be quiet and relax as you simply enjoy the presence of God. Imagine His arms of love surrounding you, holding His child tight. Thank Him for all the years He has taken care of you and done so much for you. Repeat, "Thank You, thank You, thank You." Bask in the warmth of the Light and Love which is the Eternal One. Look for any new light on your problems. Listen for anything further God wants to tell you.

Someone has written "The most important thing in any prayer is not what we say to God, but what God says to us. We are apt to pray and then hurry away without giving God a chance to answer." Doesn't that describe what we often do? In the future when you pray, stop, look and listen!

Read Isaiah 6 for a beautiful description of how all this worked in the spiritual life of the young prophet Isaiah. King Uzziah had been leading the nation of Judah for fifty-two years, guiding it to remarkable heights of prosperity and security. When Uzziah died of the dread disease, leprosy, Isaiah's whole world must have come to a screeching stop.

At prayer in the temple, Isaiah felt the foundations shake. He stopped to think about the meaning of life and cried out to God. Then his eyes were opened to the shining vision recorded in this sixth chapter of his book. And Isaiah heard the divine words that guided his life into a ministry that produced some of the most stirring words of comfort and hope ever written. Sometimes it is the devastating experiences in life that jolt us to a stop, that help us to see, and that enable us to hear the word of God.

FATHER, too often I babble on without stopping to see what You are already doing for me, without listening to what You are trying to tell me. Forgive my rudeness. Help me to be still and know that You are God. AMEN

# WAIT

*O rest in the Lord;*
*wait patiently for Him,*
*and He shall give thee*
*thy heart's desire.*
From the Oratorio *Elijah*

❀

AS I write, the trees around my Connecticut home are bare and lifeless-looking; through them I can glimpse beautiful Candlewood Lake. In a few months, the trees will be so filled with foliage that no trace of the lake will be visible. The leaves will return, but the process takes time.

So many good things take time. Whether God is building a tree, a mountain, a family, a career, or a great soul, He usually takes a good many years to do it. We need to learn to wait.

How many of Jesus' parables had to do with growth! So often His matchless stories were about a farmer sowing his grain, a tiny mustard seed growing into the largest plants, a land owner discovering that his enemy had planted weeds in his fields. "First the stalk," He said, "then the head, then the full kernel in the head." (Mark 4:28) And the process takes time.

Often when we are tempted to think our prayers are not

answered, we have not given God, or the situation, or His messengers or processes time to work. So one thing we must learn about prayer is to wait.

The Korean pastor Paul Cho tells how as a young evangelist he prayed for a bicycle to help him get about his work, for a desk to study at, and for a chair to sit in as he prepared his sermons. He pictured these items so vividly in his heart that he claimed them by faith—and grew so enthusiastic in his faith that he told his congregation that God had already given them to him. Some young men from Pastor Cho's church went with him to his room to see these new gifts from God and asked him where they were.

Cho told them, "You know before a baby is born, there are nine months of waiting before it can be seen. I have claimed these gifts by faith, but I must wait until they are visible." The youths took a story back to the congregation that the pastor was pregnant with a desk, a chair and a bicycle! But eventually his faith was vindicated; missionaries from America gave him a bicycle and he acquired the desk and chair he needed.

Then Cho prayed for a church of 10,000 members, and in time he had it. And then he asked God to make him pastor of the largest church in the world, and today he is the minister of that church, in Seoul, Korea. But he had to learn to walk the life of faith one step at a time.

Recently I watched the early-morning tide at Cape Cod. As the waves surged forward and back, I was not sure whether the tide was coming in or going out. But I waited, and before long the sand where I had been standing was covered with water, so I knew the tide was rising.

Often we must *wait* until we see the mighty tides of God exercise their awesome power.

Try these things:

Make a list of the prayer requests you have made since you started taking these seven steps to prayer power. Have any of them been answered yet? Partially answered? Have you received new light on any of the problems you have prayed about? List all these.

Set a date, a specific time for the answer to your prayer. Write it down. When the answer comes, check the date.

Try the famous "Thirty Day Experiment" pioneered by the Reverend Samuel Shoemaker. Convenant with a friend to pray for thirty days about a specific need. Keep a record of what happens during those thirty days. You may be amazed at the results!

Pray boldly, confidently, expectantly. Get rid of the barriers. Let go. Listen. And wait. God may not answer your prayers just as you wish, but answer He will. You may not recognize the answer at first. Like a wise human parent, the Father knows better than to grant us all we ask in the form we may ask it. For He cherishes for us only the best gifts.

> When I enter into God,
> All life has a meaning,
> Without asking I know;
> My desires are even now fulfilled,
> My fever is gone
> In the great quiet of God.
> My troubles are but pebbles on the road,
> My joys are like the everlasting hills.
> Walter Rauschenbusch

May the everlasting joy be yours as you wait on the Lord.

O LORD, too often I am too busy to wait for Your voice, Your will, Your answers to my prayers. Teach me Your patience. AMEN

# THE BEGINNING OF YOUR STORY

❀

R ECENTLY I saw the film *The Never Ending Story*. I liked the closing implication that you can create your own never-ending story in the magic of your mind.

Looking back over this book, I may be more conscious than you are of all that has been left unsaid. I know I have not even scratched the surface of my subject. But I hope I have suggested a few ideas that will help you a mite further along your own spiritual journey. The rest of the story of power in prayer can only be written on the pages of the rest of your life, and on into the endlessness of eternity.

And as I am sure you know, although we have talked of steps and principles, the spiritual realm is in a dimension far above what we usually mean by laws and rules. In its mysterious complexity, it flows out beyond any neat boxes we may try to confine it to. The Kingdom of God is full of endless surprises.

St. Paul prayed that his Ephesian friends might not only experience God's "incomparably great power" but also that they might have "the spirit of wisdom and revelation, so that you may know him better" and that "the eyes of your heart may be enlightened, in order that you may know the hope to which he has called you" and "the riches of his glorious inheritance." (Ephesians 1:15–19)

As we adventure in prayer, its power leads us to realize that praying is grasping the Hand that moves the world. And that knowing and loving Him is the best prize of all.

And so let us join the Apostle in these words from the majestic Letter to the Ephesians (3:20–21):

Now to him who is able to do immeasurably more than all we ask or imagine, according to his power that is at work within us, to him be glory in the church and in Christ Jesus throughout all generations, for ever and ever. AMEN

*Book design by Elizabeth Woll*
*Type set in Korinna*